PUREE COOKBOOK FOR ADULTS

The Ultimate Guide to Creating Delicious,
Nourishing Puree Meals That are Easy to Make,
And Taste Amazing Recipes

Anastasia Slater

Table of Contents

INTRODUCTION 5

CHAPTER 1 6

WHAT IS DYSPHAGIA 6
WHAT ARE THE DANGERS OF DYSPHAGIA? 7
HOW DOES PUREED FOOD HELP PEOPLE WITH
DYSPHAGIA 8

CHAPTER 2 13

HOW TO PUREE 13
HOW TO PUREE VEGETABLES 16
HOW TO PUREE POTATOES 18
HOW TO PUREE MEATS 20
HOW TO PUREE SOUPS 22
.... 22
HOW TO PUREE BREAD 27

CHAPTER 3 29

PUREED MEALS FOR ELDERLY WITH PROTEIN 29
THE BEST EQUIPMENT AND APPLIANCES FOR PUREE 33

CHAPTER 4 58

PUREED DIET RECIPES FOR DYSPHAGIA 58
PUREED DESSERT RECIPES 58
PEACH APRICOT PUREE 58
FIG BERRY PUREE 60
PEACHES AND CREAM 62
FROZEN YOGURT PARFAIT 62

PUREED RECIPES WITH PROTEIN 63

ITALIAN CHICKEN PUREE 63

SCRAMBLED EGG AND BEAN PUREE 67

PUREED EGG SALAD 68

TANGY CHICKEN SALAD 70

BASIC FISH PUREE 72

PUREED BEEF STEW 73

TUNA AND BEANS PUREE....................................... 74

CHICKEN WITH SWEET POTATO PUREE 75

SCRAMBLED EGGS 76

BOLOGNESE SAUCE... 77

PUREED SALMON 79

SAUSAGE AND ONIONS... 80

SIDE DISH AND PUREED VEGETABLE RECIPES 82

CREAMY GARLIC CAULIFLOWER PUREE 82

PUREED MACARONI AND CHEESE 84

PUREED CAULIFLOWER 85

MAPLE SWEET POTATO.. 86

CREAM OF BROCCOLI SOUP 86

PUREED SMOOTHIE RECIPES 88

BANANA PROTEIN SHAKE 88

STRAWBERRY PROTEIN SHAKE 89

CONCLUSION.. 91

Introduction

Does the concept of pureed food bring up memories of sloppy green gruel or baby food?

It shouldn't! There are numerous of methods to produce pureed meals for the elderly that are tasty and look attractive at the same time.

Making wonderful tasting pureed meals for the elderly is not difficult. But there are a few crucial stages and strategies you should know.

In this book, I am going to show you how to prepare purees that look and taste delicious.

Plus, I have included some delicious tasting pureed diet recipes and gear suggestions too!

Chapter 1

Why do Elderly People Need Pureed Food?

The major reason older individuals need their meals pureed is dysphagia which may make solid food harmful to consume in a conventional fashion.

What is Dysphagia?

The Mayo Clinic describes dysphagia as a chronic problem swallowing.

Seniors who have pain swallowing, cough or gag when swallowing, or choke regularly should consult their doctor promptly.

The most prevalent causes of dysphagia include neurological impairment from stroke, cancer, and multiple sclerosis, muscular dystrophy, and Parkinson's disease. These illnesses and disorders may affect the muscles of the throat and esophagus producing painful or difficult swallowing.

What are the Dangers of Dysphagia?

Malnutrition, Dehydration, and Loss of Weight. If you can't swallow correctly, you aren't able to obtain the nourishment and fluids intake your body requires.

Aspiration Pneumonia. This occurs when food or drink enters your airway instead of your esophagus. It may allow hazardous germs to enter the lungs and develop an illness. Pneumonia is a dangerous, often fatal, illness for the elderly.

Choking. If the meal isn't swallowed correctly, you might become choked. This might shut off your air supply leading to significant damage or even death.

How Does Pureed Food Help People with Dysphagia

Pureed food, a variant on the liquid diet for seniors, is soft food that is thinner, and simpler to swallow. Processing and mixing the meal till it is softer makes it simpler to swallow.

Sometimes, the only alternative choice is a feeding tube which is intrusive and needs surgery.

Other Conditions That Could Make Elderly People Need a Pureed Diet

Pureed food may be important if you suffer from:

• Dental issues or absence of teeth

• Dementia

• General weakness from age

It All Starts with High Quality Ingredients

Before we go into how to puree meals for the elderly, let's talk about what you purée. The components are crucial!

Good Foods to Puree

Many conventional meals may be pureed and made into soft foods including meats, vegetables, fruits, and grains.

But components that are already soft in their solid shape are the simplest to purée. If they aren't soft while raw, cook them first.

Another method is to add enough liquid to make the mixture smooth and creamy (without being watery) (without getting watery). Experiment with gravy for the main dish or ice cream or yogurt for desserts. These will add flavor to the cuisine.

• Fruit pies and cobblers puree well for a fast and simple dessert for elders. Just throw a piece in a food processor or blender — crust and all. Then combine till smooth!

• Casseroles may be pureed into a surprisingly delicious puree. Just make sure the original components are soft enough.

• Most stews and soups puree well. Usually, no more liquid is required. If there is meat in the stew, use a food processor for optimum results. Sometimes, straining is essential to get rid of lumps.

• Chicken salad and ham salad create delicious taste purees and are fast to prepare. Just throw in a blender or food processor with a little liquid. \s• Pasta salads and coleslaws also purée extremely nicely!

Foods to Avoid When Pureeing

Stay clear from meals that are overly watery, too. Drain extra liquid when possible since purees that are overly thin may potentially cause choking.

Foods that have skin that can't be removed or is too dry, will not purée properly.

Here are some foods to steer clear of while making purees:

• **Celery:** It's stringy and tough to cook effectively in a purée.

• **Nuts and Seeds:** They may easily go overlooked by the blender blades and cause choking.

• **Dried Fruit:** These may expand when they become wet, forming lumps, and are particularly difficult to incorporate entirely.

• **Beans:** They have tough skins that don't cook down soft.

• **Hard cheeses**

Vary Your Ingredients to Encourage Finicky Appetites

Also, generate variation by mixing up your components.

A pureed diet may grow old fast, but adding fresh spices and seasonings, or even new syrups or sauces, to conventional recipes can make a world of difference in a senior's pureed food diet.

Instead of drinking water for every meal, mix it up with some milk to offer protein and calcium, or fruit juices to give some vitamins and an energy boost.

You may also add liquids like aloe if they have inflammation, or nut milks to offer good fats to the diet.

Always include some fruits and veggies to every purée, if you can. Dysphagia sufferers acquire their vitamins and nutrients exclusively from what they eat as they can't necessarily swallow medications.

Chapter 2

How to Puree

Learning to create a decent puree requires practice. When you are done you should have a thick, smooth paste that contains no lumps.

But, don't be scared to experiment!

Step 1: Chop

Chop up all of the solid components first for the best results.

Any solid bits remained in the puree are highly harmful for a person suffering from dysphagia. Make sure all pieces of the mixture are cut up as tiny as possible.

Cook harder items first to make them softer.

Step 2: Puree

After your ingredients are all prepared, pour them into your pureeing appliance of choice and puree away!

Start using your device's low/slow setting. Then gradually increase the setting until it is puree.

This permits the solid bits be combined, diced, and sliced further smaller before being blended into a smooth consistency.

What Should a Puree Look Like?

• Have a smooth texture.

• Have a consistent texture throughout with no visible bumps.

• Be wet and cohesive, but not dry, sticky, crumbly, or rubbery.

• Require no chewing.

• Easy to transfer or glide to the back of the mouth, even with a weak tongue.

• Does not clump into giant sticky bits that might induce choking.

One additional method advice that I personally find quite useful is the spoon test.

When you believe you've gotten the correct texture out of the puree, take a scoop and tip it over. If the puree runs immediately off, the combination is probably too liquid for the senior to enjoy, but if it sticks on and is a touch sticky, this could be too thick for them to swallow. You want a happy medium, where the puree easily glides off of the spoon but doesn't pour like a soup.

Step 3: Strain

You want to be particularly cautious about solid bits in the final puree. Push the mixture through a fine mesh strainer with a silicone spatula to make sure the meal is very smooth and free of lumps.

Step 4: Serve

As the patient consumes the puree, make sure it's consumed carefully in little portions so that their system doesn't become overloaded.

Also, ensure sure they are sitting totally upright throughout the meal and for at least 30 minutes following. This ensures they have thoroughly digested the meal.

How Should a Puree Taste?

A purée should be tasty. It should taste as fresh as the materials used to create it.

Unless there are medical reasons not to do so, don't be scared of adding spice or a little salt or sugar to a puree.

If a puree feels boring or watery, you need a better recipe. Scroll down for some of my favorites.

Step 5: Store

To make your life simpler, try cooking huge amounts of the senior's favorite pureed food. After that, put it in containers for next meals.

To re-serve, heat the meal back up and mix it again to reconstitute it.

How to Puree Vegetables

Most veggies purée nicely and there are hundreds of recipes for them. Veggies are the major components for pureed soups, creamed soups, and ordinary purees.

Here's how to get nice pureed veggies:

1. Rough cut the veggies when raw.

2. Pre-cook before pureeing. Cook with hot liquids like milk, chicken, or vegetable stock. Don't use water — it adds no taste or nutrients to the meal. Alternately, sauté them briefly in a little butter until they start to soften. But, make sure they don't brown or build any crust on them

3. Once they mash with a fork they are ready to purée.

4. Drain the vegetables from the cooking liquid BUT preserve it in case we need to add liquid later.

5. Remove all the seeds and skins before mixing so there are no lumps.

6. Puree them in a food mill, food processor or blender.

7. Add back part of the liquid. Gradually put the retained liquid back a few spoonful at a time until you end up with a smooth, uniform puree. You might also add butter, hot milk, gravy or other smooth sauces for extra taste.

8. Thicken the purée if required. The puree may be thickened by adding additional vegetables, a little flour, or a commercial thickening

How to Puree Potatoes

Pureed potatoes are a cornerstone of a pureed diet. Here's how to get the greatest results:

• Peel potatoes fully before cooking and cut into 1″ cubes.

• Cook them in broth or even milk instead of water.

• They will mash easily with a fork when ready to purée.

• Add butter, milk, or smooth gravy to the potatoes before pureeing for extra flavor.

For the best texture, purée the potatoes using a food mill or potato ricer. A hand mixer or potato masher may also work with some effort and enough liquid.

How to Puree Meats

Protein is an essential aspect of our nutrition. But, pureed meats have a propensity to be dry and unattractive. Here are a few suggestions for preparing pureed meats that are moist and look a little more attractive.

1. Choose a Tender Cut. It'll be tougher for your blender to puree your meat if the meat is firm and hard to cut outside of the blender. This implies boneless chicken breast and better grade pieces of meat are ideal.

2. Remove Bones and Visible Fat. Chewy clumps of fat do not purée properly and might induce choking.

3. Slow Cook the Meat Whole. Next, gently simmer the meat in its natural, complete shape. This will help it keep moisture and taste. Use a cooking technique that keeps the meat wet such as boiling, steaming or stewing. Add any necessary spices or flavorings including salt and pepper.

4. Allow it to Cool. Then, after it's absolutely, properly done, refrigerate the meat for at least 2 hours or until entirely cold. This makes it easy to cut up and combine.

5. Chop it Up! Cut up the meat into tiny pieces before pureeing. This results in a purée that is more uniform.

6. Pulverize the Meat. Use a blender or food processor until you have a grain-like, almost powdery texture.

7. Add Hot Liquid and Re-blend. Then add your liquid of choice (broth, milk, gravy, etc.) but make careful to boil it up first so your puree doesn't become chilly. You'll need roughly a quarter cup of liquid for every cup of meat. Add a bit at a time to make sure you don't get it to thin.

How to Puree Soups

Pureed vegetable soups are a primary element of a pureed food diet. They are very simple to create with only a few ingredients. Here's how to create wonderful tasting pureed soup at home.

1. Choose fresh, high quality ingredients. Generally, pureed soups are created by cooking a single vegetable or

a variety of vegetables in a fat - generally butter. Just heating a few items that taste well and have strong tastes in broth or milk may produce a really tasty soup

2. Once the veggies become tender, liquid is added and the vegetables are left to simmer until soft. Broth is the most frequent liquid used for these basic soups. Chicken, vegetable, and beef stocks are available at every grocery shop. Most every home chef also has them in their cupboard. Milk or cream is another nice alternative.

3. Once the veggies are tender, it is time to purée. You may verify for correct softness by using a fork. If the meal mashes easily with a fork but the grain of the vegetable still shows, it is ready to puree. Vegetables that have overcooked and are overly soft may still be pureed. The finished soup, nevertheless, may require thickening.

4. Strain the mixture through a sieve or a colander into a big basin or pan. This manner, you may preserve the tasty cooking liquid to add back as required. Then, add the solids and a tiny quantity of the residual liquids to your puree machine of choice.

5. For a smooth puree, sift the puree to eliminate lumps and bigger particles. The majority of pureed soups can be used with the majority of kitchen strainers. Although, fine mesh strainers are better if you want a truly smooth soup.

Is the Puree Too Thick?

If the soup is too thick after pureeing, add extra liquid like cream, milk, or broth. (Don't use water – it merely dilutes the puree and doesn't provide any nutritious value.) you may need to put puree in a skillet and boil for a few minutes to reconstitute everything.

Is the Puree Too Thin?

Thin, watery soups aren't filling or attractive for most people. People suffering from dysphasia might even become choked on soups that are overly thin.

Here are techniques to thicken a pureed soup:

Flour. Simply whisk flour into an equal quantity of heated butter until mixed and add to the soup. Then mix it into the soup while cooking. This will thicken the soup as it cooks just like it does when preparing gravies and roux. The negative for flour however is it may affect the color depending on the vegetables being used. It may also lead to a glue-like consistency or top layer when the soup cools. Using flour to thicken pureed soups is the preference of most home chefs. Everyone has flour in their homes, therefore it is fast and simple to utilize this approach.

Cornstarch / Arrowroot Powder. Either of these components may be mixed into a thin paste with water then added to the pureed soup at the end. Keep the soup hot and mix the paste into the soup immediately before you serve it. Be careful: if you don't whisk it, it will clump together into really awful tasting lumps. These thickeners won't modify the color of the soup however.

Potatoes. If you know ahead of time that the soup will be thin, potatoes may make a terrific thickening. Simply peel a potato, cut into cubes, and add to the veggies while they are cooking. Then, just purée the potatoes with the veggies. Cooked rice may be utilized in the same manner.

This approach also adds nutrients and texture to a soup. And, most potatoes are light enough to not change the taste of the finished puree.

Bread. This is a popular method in exquisite french cookery. To use bread as a thickening, chop the crusts off and fry the bread (both sides) in butter until it is gently browned. After that, before the mixture is pureed, float the bread in it for a few minutes until it is soft. Finally, blend the mixture with the bread.

Egg Yolks are also used as a thickening. But this is one of the more challenging approaches. The scrambled egg yolks must be tempered to prevent ending up with scrambled eggs in the soup.

How to Puree Fruit

Pureed fruits are commonly used as a dessert or a fast snack. Both fresh fruits and canned fruits produce delicious taste purees.

1. If using fresh fruit, remove all peel, seeds, pits, and cores.

2. Make sure fresh fruits are fairly ripe.

3. Fibrous fruits (pears, apples, peaches) may need to be cooked first. If so, simmer them in apple juice or other fruit juice for the greatest flavor.

4. Canned fruits should be rinsed extremely thoroughly before pureeing.

5. Frozen fruits should be thawed entirely and also drained adequately.

6. Puree the fruit in a food mill, food processor, or blender until smooth.

7. If the puree is too thick, put back part of the original liquids or use apple juice or other fruit juice.

8. If it is too thin, add extra fruit that has been squeezed or drained. Commercial thickeners are also available.

How to Puree Bread

Did you know you can purée bread? It is for definitely one of the most challenging meals to puree and make taste and look excellent however. Properly pureed bread looks a little like pudding.

The main technique is to convert the bread product to crumbs, add warm liquid to it, and then purée together.

Don't use crusty breads — they don't purée as well and will leave lumps.

Try alternative combinations like bread crumbs with heated milk or graham cracker crumbs soaked in coffee.

Chapter 3

Pureed Meals for Elderly with Protein

When we think about purees, our attention goes to smoothies, soups, and basic liquid dishes. But high protein meals are a very essential aspect of a pureed diet since it is full and crucial to our life.

Meat

Beef. Tender top slices of beef are finest for purée. They are softer than other cuts and will mash up quicker and easier.

Chicken/Turkey. Chicken and turkey are lower fat sources of protein if you're wanting meat. Just make sure that you're obtaining boneless, skinless slices so that none of it goes into your puree.

Fish. Fish is perhaps one of the best forms of protein obtained from meat, since it comes with all sorts of additional nutrients including omega-3 fatty acids. Purees made from soft fish, such as salmon or white fish, function well. Canned seafood like tuna is another alternative.

Dairy

Milk. Milk of all sorts is rich with protein. Depending on your dietary preferences, you may want to opt for whole milk for a creamier, fattier texture to your pureed soup. You may also use skim milk for a thinner combination with just as much protein. Also check out soy milk for slightly more natural, nutritious proteins and lipids. Nut milks like cashew or almond have a lovely, mild taste.

Yogurt. Again, depending on your requirements, you can purchase yogurt with all types of variable degrees of fats, but you'll normally receive around 10-15 grams of protein per serving of yogurt. Yogurt is especially amazing since it comes in all sorts of delectable flavors — there's one for everyone!

Cheese. While not the healthiest form of protein, some varieties of soft cheeses, such cottage cheese or ricotta, are decent providers of protein. They also lend a rich, creamy texture to any purée.

Eggs. Eggs are another fantastic protein source, offering you an average of 6 grams per egg. So 2 or 3 eggs in a sitting may offer you a whooping 18 grams of protein straight immediately!

For purees, you should cook the eggs in your favorite technique (scrambled is typically simplest) before adding them to the mixture. Adding them uncooked poses the danger of not cooking them properly.

Protein Powder/Supplements

Finally, there are more protein powders and supplements created for adding to smoothies and purees than I can count.

They come in all types of tastes and textures, but virtually all of them are powdered, making them simple to add to any puree to give you a boost of protein in any meal.

There are numerous sorts of protein supplements you can acquire, from whey to soy to hemp to plant-based protein. Find what would work best with your diet and lifestyle and add a tablespoon or two to a few meals every day to acquire your appropriate protein intake.

Looking For A Ready-Made Solution?

If you are searching for an occasional, ready produced answer, check out these healthy smoothies. They have a wonderful consistency for feeding to older persons with dysphagia and may be thickened with your preferred thickener if required. I use them personally myself and can speak to how amazing they taste too!

1. Kate Farms Organic Meal Replacement Shake

These tasty and accessible plant-based shakes come in flavors (vanilla, chocolate, and coffee) with USDA Organic protein and potent phytonutrients for maximum health.

High amount of phytonutrients obtained from numerous nutrient-rich foods including green tea, acai, turmeric, and broccoli.

Reputation for employing the greatest ingredients like USDA organic pea protein for high-quality sustenance to maintain your aging body nourished, stimulated, and healthy.

It comes in three flavors: vanilla, coffee, and chocolate.

The Best Equipment and Appliances for Puree

You have so many appliance options for pureeing. Where do you even start?

Here are the most frequent ones along with some benefits and downsides of each kind. I'll also offer some suggested models for you too.

Ready? Here we go!

Best Food Processors for Purees

The common gadget most families use for pureeing meals is a food processor.

Pros

• Food processors are incredibly multipurpose, doing all types of activities from just mixing to julienning vegetables to chopping and slicing and pureeing.

• Their big basin is also typically useful for adding ingredients, and they normally feature basic, easy to use settings.

• Most feature high powered motors and big blades that make rapid work of purees.

Cons

• They tend to be on the pricey side.

• They're also enormous and heavy, so finding storage for them in your kitchen may be a pain.

• Because they are large, they may not be the greatest for little single serving pureed meals.

What's the Difference Between and Food Processor and a Blender?

The fundamental distinction between food processors and blenders is the blade. The blade is sharper on a food processor since it is meant primarily for solid foods. Blenders are best for liquids or meals with high liquid content like fruits and vegetables.

Bowl Scraper 10 Cup Food Processor by Hamilton Beach

If you require only a simple food processor for tiny pureed meals, this a perfect introduction into the food processor realm. It's an everyday food processor for pureeing vegetables, soups, and more.

It features 2 speed settings and a 450 watt motor which is the minimum motor power that I suggest for purees.

The bowl has a 10 cup capacity, a "happy medium" size, with a built in scraper. This saves time since you won't have to stop as frequently to scrape the bowl with a spatula for consistency. The feeding chute is big too.

There is also an 8 cup bowl variant available.

The stainless steel blade is what you'll use the most but there is also a stainless steel slicing disc and a shredding disc too.

The bowl, cover, and blades are also all dishwasher safe for fast and simple clean up.

The only genuine criticism about this is that it is noisy. Very loud as a matter of fact.

Cuisinart DFP-14BCWNY 14-Cup Food Processor

But if you want more power for speedier pureeing and/or want greater capacity, check out Cuisinart's 14 cup food processor. It will cost a bit extra but makes rapid work of pureeing meals.

The motor is a highly strong 720 watts for pureeing harder items like meats and other proteins.

It includes an extra big feeding tube which saves you time when producing large quantities.

It comes with the conventional S shaped blade, plus a specialist slicing disc, shredding disc, and a chopping blade too. All are composed of stainless steel for durability and cleanability. A spatula is supplied also.

All elements except for the base are dishwasher safe for simple cleaning.

Many individuals don't believe their kitchen is complete without a Kitchen Aid product in it. The brand stands on its own.

KitchenAid 11-Cup Food Processor with ExactSlice System

KitchenAid produces a pretty great food processor that allows you a lot of control over your pureeing. It is famed for its "ExactSlice" mechanism but you won't use that option much for purees.

The machine that enables you manage the speed of the blade on high, low, or pulse settings so you may vary from a thick to thin consistency. You won't find this level of control anywhere.

Here's why this is one of the finest food processors for purees: it comes with both a 9 cup and a 3 cup bowl. Small batch? Use the 3 cup to eliminate waste and achieve a smoother, more uniform puree. Larger batch? Hop up to the 9 cup bowl. This provides you numerous of alternatives with one machine.

The bowls have a tight seal feature also to avoid leaks while the machine is functioning.

You'll probably use the multipurpose blade but it does come with a reversible shredding disc and a dough blade too.

You have 4 colors to select from.

But, it is crucial to note that all of the components are suggested hand-wash only.

Best Blenders for Purees

Another typical alternative for pureeing equipment is the blender.

These too have a range of options and are quite straightforward to utilize.

Blenders are great for pureeing meals that have high liquid content like smoothies and soups.

Get one with a high powered motor for dysphagia sufferers since you'll need to mix together more solid meals, not simply fruits and vegetables for smoothies.

Take Caution Here Though!

Do not fill up the blender with hot soup — simply fill it up about a third of the way. When you turn the blender on, the hot liquid will expand and might come shooting out the top. At best, it will merely produce a mess. But, at worst, you may suffer serious burns from boiling soup flying at you. Also, wrap the lid with a dish towel and use that to keep the lid in place.

How to Use a Blender for Purees

Ok, now that you have received your blender safety instruction for the day:

1. Carefully pulse the blender to begin mixing the ingredients. This aids in preventing an explosion from the top.

2. Increase the speed to the low setting for a minute or two to further blend the meal.

3. Finally, progressively increase pace until you obtain the proper consistency.

Blenders purée food rapidly and the machine performs all the labor.

Pros of Using a Blender for Purees

• Blenders are perfect for more recipes based on liquid, such smoothies and healthy beverages. Generally, this implies they're better for pureeing too. Their blades are also highly effective, able to effortlessly shatter ice or gently mix delicate components together into a cohesive mixture as well.

For pureeing, their structure is particularly useful since with the lightweight pitcher shape and pour area that most of them come with, it's simple to transfer or pour your puree into the remainder of your combination or dish. \s• Easy to use settings, frequently coming with a defined "puree" option. Lightweight and compact structure for simple movement or storage. Wide variety of pricing to match any budget. Very adaptable for all types of blended beverages and foods.

Cons of Using a Blender for Purees

Blenders do have a few downsides.

• Blenders aren't good with more solid meals. They tend to clog up.

• Also, you sometimes have to work in bunches which may not save time. However, for a few portions of a pureed soup, a blender may work fairly well.

•Not excellent for huge or bulk cooking, since the largest blenders normally contain approximately 11 cups.

•If you are using a blender to purée meats, you will want to acquire one with loads of power.

Here are my suggestions for the best blenders for pureeing food.

Ninja BL610 Black 1000-watt Professional Blender

The Ninja BL610 is my personal fave.

While the Ninja blender is on the pricey side, you won't regret your purchase. It gives superb control, with low, medium and high settings. You'll love the exceptionally rapid performance from the 1000 watt motors.

The Total Crushing Blades can quickly crush anything, including ice and fruit that is being softly pureed. Plus, it has a vast capacity to fulfill all your meal demands.

The blades are particularly developed Total Crushing Blades that can break fruits, vegetables and ice with ease. You may use it at 3 different speeds and a pulse function. It is pretty loud though.

All pieces are also BPA free and dishwasher safe for extra convenience.

Ninja Nutri Ninja PRO Pulse Blender

If the Ninja Professional is too large for you, this one is a fantastic solution.

This Amazon Best Seller features a tiny footprint that doesn't take up a lot of room. Yet it still has a very strong 900w motor.

It comes with two cups (18oz and 24oz in size) with lids for each for simple storing.

The Nutri Ninja breaks everything down meals simply. This blender is perfect for producing one serve puree from softened veggies or other ingredients.

The negative unfortunately is that the jars are not heat resistant. So, you will need to wait for food to cool down before blending it in this blender.

NutriBullet Balance Blender

Want more power? This Nutribullet blender comes with an excellent 1700w engine. This strong equipment is able to process a lovely smooth puree.

On the other hand, there is a substantial variation in price, so you have to bear that in mind.

This blender comes with 3 containers, a 34oz pitcher, a 32oz small cup and a 45oz big cup. Each container comes with a storage cover also.

Another bonus for this one is that it can work with hot meals. It also has built-in heating feature. The motor is pretty noisy however. The Nutribullet could even slide a little bit across the surface while it works!

Cleaning is a little more challenging and is best done by hand.

Best Blender For Pureeing Meat

But, what about meat?

Well, you need sharp blades and plenty of force to purée meats. These blenders are great for pureeing meat and proteins.

Vitamix Professional Grade Blender (5200)

Vitamix machines, particularly this one, are tremendously powerful. It receives amazing ratings online by users, one going so far as to declare "this isn't a blender — it's a way of life." It's so strong that it can combine everything from nuts to coffee beans to dough and yes, even flesh.

This blender includes a huge 64 ounce container which is perfect for large meals or if you prefer to create large amounts and then put them away.

It also boasts a simple to use, comprehensive control dial adjustment function that works while it's mixing, so you're always in control of the process.

The blades themselves are stainless steel, and can really reach speeds so high that they cause friction heat. This means you can take cold components (such meat) and actually cook them into a lovely blended soup in approximately 6 minutes using this machine.

Of course, it is a Vitamix so you will pay extra for it due of the brand, reputation, and features.

Honestly speaking, high powered food processors like the ones above will purée tough meat items better.

Best Immersion Blenders for Pureeing Food

An immersion blender is the portable version of the blender that sits on your countertop.

It features a rotating blade on one end of the shaft with controls on the other end. Most connect into an electric socket but there are battery operated variants also.

How to Make Purees with an Immersion Blender

To use an immersion blender,

1. Chop the meal into extremely tiny pieces.

2. Cook the items in liquid until soft in a big saucepan.

3. Then, drop the handheld blender down into the meal ensuring sure you are holding it level.

4. Turn it on and begin moving it around in the meal. You'll feel a suction which will assist maintain the blender head flat on the bottom.

5. You'll have to pick it up regularly after shutting it off to make sure you got all the food item pureed.

Using an Immersion Blender for Purees Has Many Benefits

• They operate as all-in-one, portable, handheld replacements to blenders, food processors, and more.

•They're quite straightforward to use, generally featuring a one touch mechanism that switches the machine on or off. Just put all of your ingredients into a saucepan or container, insert the immersion blender, and go! You'll get a wonderful puree, smoothie, sauce, or perhaps a silky smooth soup in seconds.

• Another, probably even more tempting, characteristic is their price. They're frequently far more cheap than their bigger equivalents.

Cons of Making Purees with an Immersion Blender

• First, the food must be pre-chopped into tiny bits or the blender head would clog. This may generate a lumpy puree.

• Second, they don't play good with certain enamel pans. If the blender has a stainless steel head or the blade is rotated at an angle, it may harm the enamel pan surface.

• Finally, make sure you keep control of the blender. If you let it get away from you, you'll have puree all over your stove and kitchen!

Cuisinart CSB-175 Smart Stick Hand Blender

Don't let the price tag mislead you. The Cuisinart immersion blender is one of the most powerful on the list and doesn't sacrifice quality for cost.

It includes a detachable shaft that's simple to remove and dishwasher safe for easy cleaning. It's also constructed out of stainless steel which is incredibly robust and won't stain. To shield your hands and fingers from the powerful blade, the body of this immersion blender has a built-in blade guard.

It also comes in 10 various colors, so you can pick and choose what would best complement your kitchen's design!

Inkbird Immersion Hand Blender

If you want to kick your immersion blender pick up a notch without breaking the wallet, try out Epica's model.

It includes a very ordinary 350 watt motor and good grade stainless steel blades. But it's also really simple to use with a one click release for your attachments (it comes with conventional mixer and whisk attachments) (it comes with standard mixer and whisk attachments).

All of these pieces are dishwasher safe, too.

The biggest feature of this machine is its variable speed dial which provides you total control over the power and speed of your blender. This is a unique function that's uncommon to find in inexpensive immersion blenders.

It also comes with a variety of wonderful attachments, including a 3 cup blending and storage jar with graded markings, a suction cover, and pouring spout, and a 2 cup chopping bowl for solid materials.

This is one of the greatest, and most adaptable selections available on the list.

BELLA Hand Immersion Blender (14460)

This immersion blender is the most cheap on the list coming in at around $20.

You may question what makes this model so inexpensive but it's really a pretty excellent quality blender for its price.

Of course, it's not nearly as high powered as others with only a 250 watt motor and one speed.

But, it will still work for smaller amounts of soft sauces or meals if that's what you mostly intend to use your immersion blender for.

Both the 6 inch blending attachment and a replaceable whisk are constructed out of stainless steel. Both of the accessories are dishwasher safe, as well.

You'll also enjoy the gently covered, ergonomic handle. It's a terrific deal if you don't require a high-powered, high performance machine.

Best Food Mills for Smooth Pureed Food

Food mills are an exceptionally handy equipment for creating purees. Additionally, there's a chance you've never heard of them.

Meal processors and blenders literally crush the food into nothingness. While that may be great occasionally, other times you may prefer a very thick texture that's evocative of actual food.

So, what is a food mill?

A food mill is simply a grinder and a strainer combined into one. You just place the softened food in the top and then turn the handle. This drives the food through the grinder disks and while straining it at the same time. You end up with a wonderful, silky purée on one side and all the seeds and skins on the other.

Because food mills accomplish the function of two separate kitchen items, utilizing a food mill saves you precious time. And, I believe, you end up with a superior puree if you are going for an ultra-smooth, velvety feel.

Pros of Making Purees with a Food Mill

• Creates a flawless puree texture while filtering away any undesirable bits.

• It doesn't consume energy and is quite self-explanatory to operate.

Cons of Making Purees with a Food Mill

• Manual operation may be difficult for certain persons to handle.

• They need installation and disassembly every time they are used or cleaned

OXO Good Grips Food Mill

The OXO food mill is probably the finest food mill for pureed foods.

The grinding discs swap in and out rapidly using a quick-release clasp. There are 3 sizes too: fine (1 mm), medium (3 mm), and coarse (8 mm) (8 mm).

The 1 mm disc is the smallest on the market and works excellent for ultra smooth purees like baby food or a bowl of red tomato sauce.

It's 3 mm disc is the size you will use most and is fantastic for mashed potatoes and vegetable purees.

The OXO is also the only one that features a disc as big as 8 mm. This is the appropriate size for chunkier soups and sauces.

This food processor is quite stable also. There are three small legs on the bottom that are covered with rubber. These feet function like tripods and support the mill on top of the bowl to prevent it from wobbling around while you are grinding away. They also fold in for simple storage.

The key characteristic of the OXO Good Grips range is the comfy handles. They are bigger than many other handles and are also soft and flexible. This makes them simple to grasp onto without needing to squeeze too hard. A great benefit for individuals with arthritis.

Both the mill itself and the discs are constructed of stainless steel which will endure for years with careful maintenance. It will also hold up to frequent usage with hot liquids and meals.

Finally, it comes apart fast for complete cleaning and is dishwasher safe on the top rack.

Alisa Home Foley Food Mill

I also highly appreciate and suggest this food mill from Alisa Home for those searching for a simple unit for occasional usage.

It is a beautifully designed and surprisingly sturdy food grinder that is virtually ideal.

Almost. If it was simply stainless steel that is.

The plastic bowl is the sole disadvantage of this model. But that may not be a significant concern to certain people. The plastic bowl does have one significant benefit though: it is lighter than a stainless steel one. This might make it simpler for certain folks to use and maintain. For those concerned about BPA, this product is certified BPA-free.

The Alisa Home mill does have certain stability elements incorporated in it like the notched feet. There are small grooves on the underside of the feet that assist grab the edge of the bowl. These restrict the mill from moving about so much when it is being utilized.

Like the previous versions, this mill features 3 removable discs in fine, medium, and coarse. The discs shift in and out quite easy by popping in and out of the lip on the plastic basin. Then, the grinding handle is reattached to the middle hole.

The Alisa Home mill is also dishwasher safe on the top rack and disassembles simply for cleaning.

Almost everybody can afford this well-priced food grinder. You can generally pick one up for less than $30.00.

Weston Stainless Steel Food Mill

For an entry-level, cheaper food mill, the Weston food mill is a good product.

It does have all the normal features like 3 sizes of milling discs, a stainless steel bowl, and it is simple to clean.

However, there is a fundamental difficulty with this food mill that has to do with stability.

Stability, as I spoke about earlier, is vital when utilizing a food mill. Otherwise, you might wind up with a large mess.

This food mill, regrettably, lies loosely on top of the bowl while being used. Another alternative is to hold it firmly with one hand over the top of the bowl. Neither of these fixes offers the same level of security as the OXO's tripod feet or the Alisa model's notched feet. This implies that the food mill is likely to move about – a lot – while being utilized.

Favorite Potato Ricers for Purees and Mashed Potatoes

Potato ricers may be the one thing here you haven't heard much about. They are often used with potatoes and other root vegetables.

Potato ricers essentially look like a giant garlic crusher. A screen with holes the size of rice grains is located on the bottom. A pusher then presses the food through the openings so that you end up with what appears like fluffy mashed potatoes.

Pros of Making Purees with a Potato Ricer

• Creates the best, creamiest, richest texture for purees.

• They're also reasonably economical, don't consume any additional power, and they are straightforward to operate.

Cons of Making Purees with a Potato Ricer

• Requires a lot of human effort.

• It also has a fairly restricted usage, you can really only use a potato ricer for a number of meals, so it may spend a lot of time in storage.

•You also have to add a few stages to the procedure to achieve your puree.

OXO Good Grips 3-in-1 Adjustable Potato Ricer

OXO's potato ricer features a conventional, handheld build and functions excellently. It features a sturdy stainless steel body for assured performance, yet the handles are covered with a soft substance, making it incredibly simple to use. It also contains knobs on each end that prevent it from sliding into the bowl, which is a really unique feature.

Other Suggested Equipment for Making Purees

A Good Rubber Spatula

This is more significant than you may know. Trying to scrape pureed food out of a dish with a metal spoon is tough and irritating.

Get an excellent rubber or silicone spatula that has a smooth, flat edge. This will make scraping dishes much simpler. Another advantage is you'll be able to get most of the puree out of the bowl which lowers waste and cleans up easily.

I like this set since it is heat resistant and comes with many sizes.

Silicone Spatula 14-piece Set

Strainer

Strainers are vital to pureeing particularly if you do not have a reliable food mill. Using food processors and blenders for purees might create an uneven final result. Sometimes fibrous foods will not purée fully. Perhaps seeds or skins found their way into the finished product.

A strainer can help remove them from your purée. You set the strainer over a big bowl and shove the purée through with you trusty rubber spatula. This will trap the bigger particles on one side and enable a smooth, velvety puree to pour out the other.

Strainers come with varied sized mesh. A regular metal kitchen strainer will work for most individuals. If you require an extremely smooth purée, purchase a fine mesh strainer.

Chapter 4

Pureed Diet Recipes for Dysphagia

Looking for fantastic tasting quick recipes for a pureed? Here are some favorites!

Pureed Dessert Recipes

Peach Apricot Puree

This puree has a fantastic blend of sweet and sour. The inclusion of oats also provides some bulk for a heartier puree that will help you feel full longer.

Ingredients

• 2 pounds frozen peaches

• 8 oz dried apricots

- 2 cup apple juice no-sugar added, organic is better

- 2/3 cup quick 1 minute oats

- 1 tbsp cinnamon

Instructions

1. Dump the frozen peaches, apricots, and apple juice into a saucepan

2. Turn up to high until mixture begins boiling

3. Simmer on high for 5 minutes stirring occasionally \s4. Add oats, mix well, and boil another minute

5. Put contents of saucepan in blender. (CAUTION while mixing hot floodwaters, never fill the blender to more than half way. The food will expand while bending and you might wind up with hot puree blasting out of the tip of the blender! Make sure the lid is on securely and throw a cloth over it for safety.)

6. Blend until absolutely smooth (2-3 minutes)

Fig Berry Puree

The figs in this puree give a little acidity to the sweetness of the strawberries and apple juice. Finishing it up with some ground cloves provides a festive holiday atmosphere.

Ingredients

• 2 pound frozen strawberries

- 8 oz dried figs

- 1 cup apple juice no-sugar added, organic is better

- 1 cup fast, 1 minute oats

- 1 tsp ground cloves

Instructions

1. Cut the figs in half and remove any stem from the pointy end of the fig.

2. If using fresh strawberries, remove the top and bottom and cut in half also.

Cooking

1. Add the strawberries, figs, and apple juice to a saucepan

2. fig berry puree recipe items put to a pan

3. Turn heat on high and cover

4. Once boiling begins, cook for 5 minutes stirring once

5. Add the oats, stir and simmer for another minute

6. Remove from heat and pour contents of the pan plus the powdered cloves to a blender (CAUTION while

mixing hot foods. Do not load your blender beyond half way or hot food might be blasted out the top of it. Make sure the lid is secure and lay a cloth on top for added protection)

7. Blend until smooth (2-3 minutes) (2-3 minutes)

Peaches and Cream

For a fast and easy dessert:

1. Strain one jar of baby peaches.

2. Add one cup of ice cream, a dash of nutmeg and 1/8 of a teaspoon vanilla essence.

3. Blend until smooth.

Frozen Yogurt Parfait

This may be used as a breakfast or dessert item.

• Puree together vanilla yogurt with your seniors' favorite fruits and a little of almond milk.

•Serve as is or freeze overnight to produce a delightful, nutritious ice-cream like dessert.

Pureed Recipes with Protein

Italian Chicken Puree

Slightly acidic pureed chicken with loads of Italian flavor.

Ingredients:

- 1/2 cup cooked chicken

- 3 tablespoons tomato sauce

- 1-1/2 teaspoon Italian seasoning

- Salt and pepper to taste

Instructions

1. Use a food processor or blender to combine all the ingredients. You might also combine them by hand using a fork.

2. Once the mixture is completely combined and soft, microwave it for 30 seconds.

Dish Notes

- Use left-over cooked chicken breasts or tenders for this recipe.

- Canned chicken may also be used for a fast and simple puree.

Black Bean and Red Pepper Puree

A extremely healthy puree for the mexican cuisine enthusiast particularly. Expect a little amount of heat with this one.

Ingredients

- 1 cup black beans washed and drained

- 3 tablespoons enchilada sauce

- 4 tablespoons chopped roasted red pepper

- 3 tablespoons chicken broth

Instructions

1. Place the beans, half the enchilada sauce and peppers in a skillet and cook over medium heat.

2. When these items are cooked, add the chicken broth.

3. Turn off the heat and combine the ingredients, using an immersion or normal blender.

4. Transfer the puree to a serving dish, and add the remaining half of the enchilada sauce before serving.

Recipe Notes

- You can purchase red peppers already cooked in the condiment aisle, deli, or Mexican sections of most supermarket stores.

- Garnish this with a little guacamole (finely blended) or sour cream to complete the Mexican theme.

Scrambled Egg and Bean Puree

A easy recipe for a breakfast puree with loads of protein that would make a fantastic supper too.

Ingredients

For the scrambled eggs:

• 1 egg

• Salt and pepper

For the bean puree:

• 1/2 cup black beans washed and drained

• 3 tablespoons enchilada sauce

• 2 tablespoons broth

Instructions

For the black bean puree:

1. Place the beans and enchilada sauce in a skillet and cook over medium heat.

2. After around 2 minutes, add the broth of your liking.

3. Use an immersion or conventional blender to puree the mixture, and serve it in a dish.

4. Alternatively, you may prepare the bean puree in advance put it in the freezer until you cook the eggs.

For the scrambled eggs:

1. Heat a pan or skillet and whisk your eggs in a bowl before placing them into the pan.

2. Add salt and pepper to taste, and be sure to stir the eggs with a spatula while they cook.

3. When they have achieved the proper consistency, remove them from the fire and serve them with the bean puree and enchilada sauce.

Recipe Notes \s• A wonderful garnish for this can be sour cream or finely pureed guacamole.

Pureed Egg Salad

This is the pureed version of the lumpy sandwich filling you've undoubtedly had before. Don't like olives? You may replace the more conventional pickles or pickle relish instead.

Ingredients

- 2 hard-boiled egg

- 1-1/2 tablespoon green onion chopped

- 2 tablespoon tomatoes diced

- 2 tablespoon soft cheese cottage, ricotta, or feta are best
- 1 teaspoon olives sliced (optional)

- 2 teaspoon reduced-fat mayonnaise

- Salt and pepper to taste

Instructions

1. In a bowl, combine all the ingredients except the cheese.

2. Use a food processor or blender to mix until you obtain a creamy consistency.

3. Gently whisk in the cheese and serve cold.

Recipe Notes

If you have difficulties peeling your eggs after boiling them, add a teaspoon of baking soda to the water before boiling.

You may also purchase eggs already hard boiled at the supermarket store although they tend to be a little rubbery. If you take this way, make sure they purée thoroughly.

Tangy Chicken Salad

This chicken salad dish has a somewhat acidic taste to it but is primarily bland — and that's on design! It is a fantastic dish for introducing back meats and proteins to a diet after bariatric surgery or for dysphagia. Increasing or adding spice is easy to do afterwards.

Ingredients

- 1 cup cooked or canned chicken

- 2 tbsp Greek yogurt

- 2 tablespoon reduced-fat mayonnaise

- 1/2 teaspoon onion powder

- Salt & Pepper to taste

Instructions

1. Place the chicken into a food processor and grind it until it is smooth.

2. Add in the yogurt, mayonnaise, salt, pepper, and onion powder and blend until smooth

3. Garnish with chives if desired.

Dish Notes

Freshly cooked chicken is excellent for this recipe but not usually accessible.

I like to reserve chicken tenders from previous dinners for this.

Remember to chop up the chicken in very little pieces before pureeing.

If you use canned chicken, rinse it a bit to eliminate any salt.

Canned chicken will sometimes puree easier since it is already in smaller parts.

Basic Fish Puree

This is simply a basic, fast, and easy fish puree recipe. You can use leftover freshly cooked fish for this or make it fairly simple with canned tuna or salmon.

Ingredients

- 1 cup cooked or tinned fish tuna or salmon, drained well
- 1 tablespoon reduced-fat mayonnaise
- 1 tablespoon green onions chopped
- Salt and pepper to taste

Instructions

1. Place the cooked or tinned fish in a food processor, and process until it becomes smooth.

2. Place in a bowl and whisk with the mayonnaise, salt, and pepper.

3. Garnish with freshly sliced green onions.

Pureed Beef Stew

This is a more handmade alternative. You can also purée canned beef stew also directly out of the can for a speedy lunch.

Ingredients:

• Tender Cut of Beef, Diced

• Bag of Frozen Peas, Carrots, etc.

• Beef Broth or Gravy

• Salt & Pepper

Instructions:

1. Cook four ounces of beef until tender.

2. Boil favorite veggies such as carrots and peas until soft.

3. Add half a cup of beef stock or gravy.

4. Blend together until you get the desired consistency.

Tuna and Beans Puree

Besides being protein filled, tuna fish has numerous additional advantages owing to its vitamins, minerals and other chemical substances. It is possible to minimize cardiovascular disease, boost muscular development and lower blood pressure. On the other hand, white beans are fiber-rich and an excellent source of magnesium. When combined, these two components produce for a delectable purée.

Ingredients:

- 15 oz beans, canned or cooked till soft

- 1 small can of tuna

- Lemon juice from ½ lemon

- Pinch of basil

- Salt to taste

Preparation:

1. Blend each item in a food processor until completely smooth.

2. If the puree is too thick you may add little water.

Chicken with Sweet Potato Puree

Chicken breast is noted for its high protein value, at 31%. In addition to protein, chicken is a good source of minerals and the vitamins B3, B5, B6, and D. Sweet potatoes, rich in vitamin A, fiber and potassium, are an excellent ingredient to produce an amazing puree.

Ingredients:

• 6 oz chicken breast, skinless and boneless

• 12 ounces sweet potato, peeled and cubed \s• Salt and additional spices to taste

Preparation:

1. Cook chicken in a small pot in boiling water for approximately 15 minutes or until flesh is done. Remove from water, let it cool.

2. Cook the sweet potato in a saucepan in boiling water until very tender. Drain the potatoes, but save the liquid.

3. Put chicken, potatoes, seasonings and a tiny quantity of cooking liquid in a food processor, and blend it until smooth. Add extra water if too thick.

Scrambled Eggs

If you are on a pureed diet, scrambled eggs are a fantastic alternative. Egg proteins are readily digested and are used as a benchmark to test protein quality in meals. Eggs are a great source of minerals, vitamins A and B complex, and proteins.

Here is a simple scrambled egg puree recipe. As an addition to this simple dish, you may saute chopped onions, mushrooms or ham over some butter before frying the eggs and then blend everything in a food processor. You may also add some shredded cheese to the eggs.

Ingredients:

• 2 eggs

• 3 oz of milk

• Salt

• Pepper

Preparation:

1. Mix 2 eggs, salt, pepper and 1 oz milk in a small basin.

2. Cook the eggs in a pot over low to medium heat.

3. Stir well while cooking, be cautious not to overcook.

4. Place the ingredients in a food processor or blender, add the remaining 2 oz of milk and pulse until smooth.

Bolognese Sauce

A classic that pairs wonderfully with vegetable puree, for example mashed potatoes. Beef meat used in this dish includes 26% of protein in a piece of meat, which means it fits nicely in your protein-rich diet. Be free to adapt the following recipe to your personal taste.

Ingredients:

- ½ tablespoon sunflower oil

- 1 oz onion (chopped)

- 1 oz carrots (chopped)

- 3 oz minced beef

- 1 tablespoon tomato puree

- 1 cup beef stock

- ½ garlic

- Pinch of oregano

Preparation:

1. Heat the oil in a skillet, and sauté the onions and carrots for a few minutes.

2. When tender, add the minced meat and tomato puree and cook for a few more minutes.

3. Add garlic and oregano, pour the stock and bring to a boil.

4. Cook for around 40 minutes.

5. Let it cool a little, put the sauce in a food processor and combine.

Pureed Salmon

A fish that is a favorite to many. It is fantastic taste and rich in vital amino-acids. It contains about 20% protein content, which is good. I am giving a simple salmon puree recipe which won't disappoint.

Ingredients:

- ½ cup water

- ½ ounce dry white wine

- 1 ounce onion, sliced

- ½ lemon, sliced

- 1 ½ teaspoon salt

- 2 springs parsley (no stems)

- 2 springs dill (no stems)

- 3 oz boneless and skinless salmon steaks

- 1 oz cream

Preparation:

1. Put water, wine, onion, lemon, salt, pepper, parsley and dill in a pot.

2. Heat until it boils, then decrease heat, cover and simmer for 10 minutes.

3. Add the salmon steaks, cover the pot and cook for 5 minutes or until fish flakes easily.

4. Pour cream to the mixture and blend in a food processor.

Sausage and Onions

Possibly not as healthful as other recommendations, but wonderful taste anyway. When picking which sausage to purchase, try to pick out ones that have more meat and lower fat percentage, since some might be overfilled with fat.

Ingredients:

• 3 oz of sausage meat or peeled uncooked sausage \s• 2 oz onions

• ½ cup water

• 1 teaspoon gravy browning

• 1 teaspoon chopped sage

Preparation:

1. Put the sausage, onions, water and sage into a skillet and simmer for 10 minutes.

2. Let it cool a little, add the gravy browning and mix until smooth.

3. If you prefer, you might add tomato sauce, white sauce or gravy, or mustard to the mix to create varied tastes.

Side Dish and Pureed Vegetable Recipes

Creamy Garlic Cauliflower Puree

This puree is an excellent option for mashed potatoes for anyone trying to cut their carbohydrates or want to mix things up a bit.

Ingredients

- 2 cup cauliflower cut and cooked

- 1 bulb garlic smashed and peeled \s• 2 tablespoon nonfat buttermilk

- 1 tablespoon soft cheese cottage, ricotta, or feta

- 2 teaspoon olive oil

- Salt and pepper to taste

Instructions

1. Chop cauliflower into 1″ pieces and boil for approximately 10 minutes - until easily mashed with a fork.

2. Place all the ingredients in a food processor and pulse until the texture is smooth and creamy.

3. You may add cottage, ricotta or feta cheese if you desire to do so.

4. Serve in a dish and garnish with chives, if preferred.

Recipe Notes \s• Whole milk or half & half are absolutely excellent alternatives for the buttermilk. They will have a bit less sour taste too.

• Careful with the cheese addition — certain persons with dysphagia should not consume cheese owing to the danger of choking.

Pureed Macaroni and Cheese

Ingredients:

• Boxed Macaroni and Cheese Kit

• Milk

Instructions:

1.As usual, prepare your favorite Mac and cheese.

2. Put 1 cup of the cooked Mac and Cheese to a blender.

3. Add 1 cup of milk.

4. Blend in a blender until smooth.

Pureed Cauliflower

I prepare this dish for myself and my kids also as lower carb alternate to mashed potatoes. I add a little garlic too.

Ingredients:

• 1 Head of Cauliflower, Chopped

• Water

• Butter

• Salt & Pepper

Instructions:

1. Boil the cauliflower until extremely soft. Save half a cup of the cooking liquid when it's done.

2. Put the cauliflower in the blender with the boiling water.

3. Add salt and pepper to taste.

4. Add a tiny quantity of butter to taste.

5. Blend until smooth.

Maple Sweet Potato

Ingredients:

• Sweet Potato, Peeled and Diced

• Cream or Milk, 1 Tbsp

• Maple Syrup, 2 tsp

• Butter, 2 tsp

• Cinnamon, sprinkle

Instructions:

1. Boil or microwave the sweet potato until tender.

2. Put potato in blender or food processor.

3. Add the cream or milk, syrup, butter, and cinnamon.

4. Blend thoroughly.

Cream of Broccoli Soup

Ingredients:

• Butter, 2 Tbsp

- Oil, 2 Tbsp

- Flour, 2 -3 Tbsp

- Milk, 1 Cup

- Bag of Frozen Broccoli

- Soft Shredded Cheese, ¼ cup

- Potato Flakes (if required for thickening)

Instructions:

1. Create a thick soup foundation by mixing together two teaspoons of butter, two tablespoons of oil, and two to three tablespoons of flour depending on your desired thickness.

2. Heat on low until the mixture starts to boil while stirring constantly.

3. Slowly mix in one cup of skim milk.

4. Allow fresh mixture to boil until it thickens.

5. While waiting, cook the broccoli in the microwave until warm and tender. Chop into smaller pieces if required.

6. Puree this base with a cup of cooked broccoli and ¼ cup of shredded cheese of your preference. An immersion blender or normal blender works well.

7. Add potato flakes to thicken, if required.

Pureed Smoothie Recipes

Banana Protein Shake

In addition to the natural protein sources, we may ingest protein in powder form. The one utilized in this recipe, and also perhaps the most common one is whey protein. It is a milk protein and it is naturally isolated as a by-product of producing cheese. It is particularly beneficial as it includes all 9 necessary amino acids.

Ingredients:

• 1 cup almond milk

• 1 cup plan Greek yogurt

• 1 scoop vanilla protein powder

- 1 frozen banana (not essential to be frozen, but offers a nicer texture) \s• ⅛ teaspoon ground cinnamon

- ice

Preparation:

1. Add almond milk, Greek yogurt, banana and cinnamon into a blender.

2. Blend until smooth.

3. If the shake is too thick, you may add some more almond milk to the blender.

Strawberry Protein Shake

Another healthy dish utilizing whey protein as an ingredient. If you want some diversity you should try this one, it is wonderful and has enough protein to maintain your diet.

Ingredients:

- ½ cup almond milk

- ¼ cup Greek yogurt

- 3 strawberries, fresh or frozen

- ½ scoop vanilla whey protein powder

- 3 ice cubes

- Stevia or honey to taste

Preparation:

1. Blend together all the ingredients.

2. Blend until smooth.

3. Add almond milk if mix is too thick.

conclusion

As you become older, changes in your body may make eating more challenging. Sometimes, accidents and medical disorders take away your capacity to swallow safely.

This is unhealthy for the elderly and may lead to inadequate nutrition for our senior loved ones. But, even confronted with that truth, some individuals refuse to move to pureed meals in the notion that they taste and look unpleasant.

Pureed food doesn't have to be that much different from solid meals.

Just make several of your favorite dishes as usual and enjoy them in a blended version. Use high walled or partitioned plates to protect meals from running together. If the older person has difficulties using standard utensils, check out these simple to use forks and spoons. Use adult-sized sippy cups for sipping liquid meals.

So if you struggle to consume conventional meals, for whatever reason, don't be scared to try pureed foods. With a little bit of skill and the correct methods, you can produce healthy pureed food that looks,

Made in the USA
Las Vegas, NV
16 January 2024

84437539R00056